52 THINGS TO DO WHILE YOU POO

HUGH JASSBURN

 sourcebooks

Published by Sourcebooks, Inc.

P.O. Box 4410, Naperville, Illinois 60567-4410

(630) 961-3900

Fax: (630) 961-2168

www.sourcebooks.com

Originally published in 2013 in the United Kingdom by Summersdale Publishers Ltd.

Printed and bound in the United States of America.

VP 10 9 8 7 6 5 4

TO MY WIFE AND KIDS, FOR ALWAYS
BEING THERE, UNTIL THEY HAD TO
LEAVE THE ROOM

HUGH JASSBURN HAS BEEN POOING SINCE 1974. AFTER SEVERAL MONTHS OF PRODUCING A VARIETY OF STOOLS (MOSTLY IN WASHABLE AND REUSABLE DIAPERS), HE MOVED ON TO DISPOSABLES. BY 1978 HUGH WAS A REGULAR TOILET USER AND HASN'T LOOKED BACK SINCE. HIS FAVORED POSITION IS WITH HIS BACK TO THE CISTERN, BOTH FEET PLANTED FIRMLY ON THE GROUND, AND BOTH ELBOWS RESTING ON HIS KNEES. HE FLUSHES WHEN HE'S STANDING, IS NOT A FAN OF CHEAP TOILET PAPER, AND STRONGLY BELIEVES THE FLAP SHOULD ALWAYS BE AT THE FRONT OF THE ROLL.

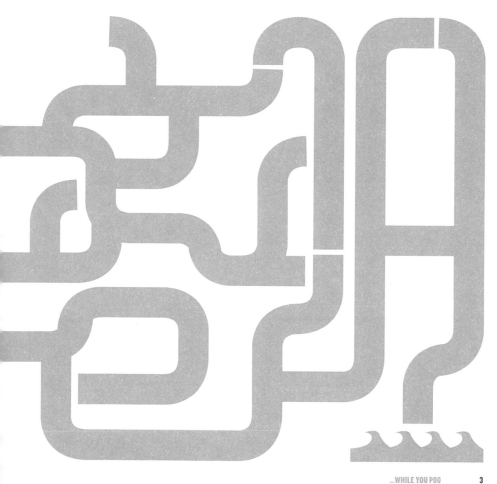

70% WATER

10% INDIGESTIBLE FOOD
10% DEAD BACTERIA
10% FATS, SALTS, LIVE BACTERIA, DEAD CELLS, MUCUS

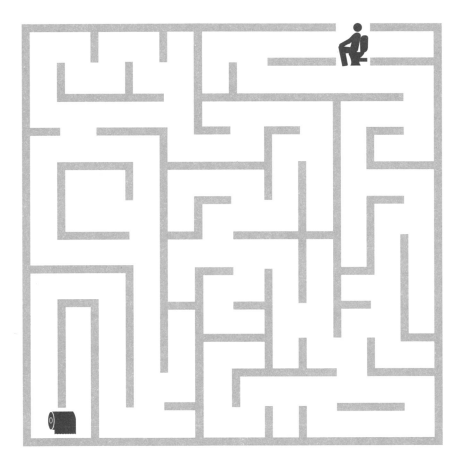

THIS PAIR ONLY APPEARS **ONCE**
ON THE NEXT PAGE.

72.4%

27.6%

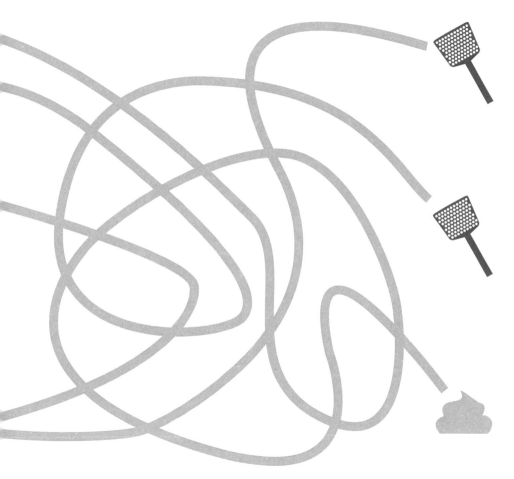

POO
FACT

WOMEN ARE
MORE LIKELY TO
SCRUNCH THE
TOILET PAPER.
MEN TEND TO BE
FOLDERS.

A RAT CAN SURVIVE AFTER BEING FLUSHED DOWN A TOILET. IT CAN OFTEN COME BACK THE SAME WAY.

THE FIRST CUBICLE IN
A PUBLIC BATHROOM IS
THE LEAST USED—IT IS
ALSO THE CLEANEST.

POO

CRAP

DROPPING

STOOL

DUMP

MUCK

NUMBER TWO

SHIT

EXCREMENT

TURD

CACA

FAECES

```
F A E C E S D U M P
H N L B E S R O U A
S U C U X Q O O C J
S M A O C R P T K B
T B C C R A P Y O S
O E A N E Z I N P H
O R R E M A N D O I
L T G I E P G V O T
E W H I N M A L I P
F O T K T U R D M V
```

WHOSE POO?

FIND THE VACANT TOILET

SPOT THE DIFFERENCE—THERE'S ONLY ONE!

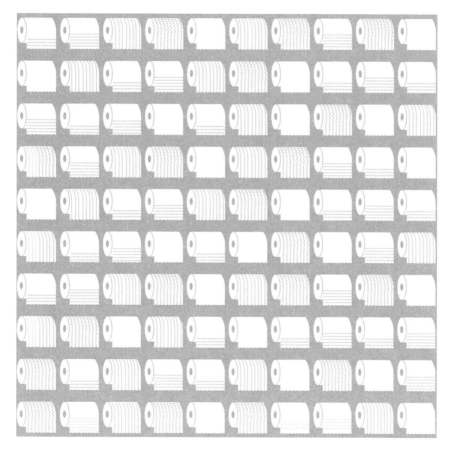

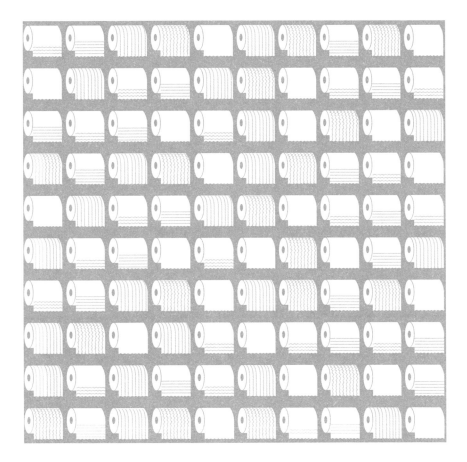

THE FLUSH HANDLE IN A
PUBLIC BATHROOM CAN HAVE
UP TO 40,000 GERMS PER
SQUARE INCH.

MOST TOILETS FLUSH
IN THE KEY OF E FLAT.

WHOSE POO?

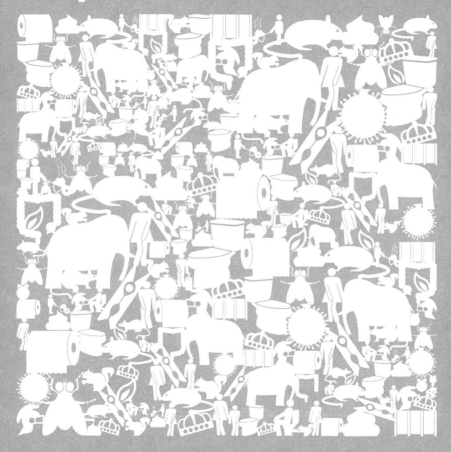

POO SMELLS DUE TO THE
SULPHUR-RICH COMPOUNDS
INDOLE, SKATOLE, MERCAPTANS,
AND HYDROGEN SULPHIDE GAS.

THE FIRST ATTEMPTS
AT MAKING TOILET AIR
FRESHENERS WERE
POMEGRANATES STUDDED
WITH CLOVES.

TOILET
OUTHOUSE
LAVATORY
BOG
DUNNY
RESTROOM
KHAZI
PRIVY
JOHN
CAN
THRONE

```
A Q R Y J O H N Z M
I W E P N N Y U L L
B G S O T D V C A N
O U T H O U S E V T
G B R J I N S J A H
X C O R L N Y I T R
D E O S E Y P K O O
T A M I T K Z H R N
P R O U P R I V Y E
N I A P K H A Z I G
```

COMPLETE THE SEQUENCE

ONE   TWO   THREE

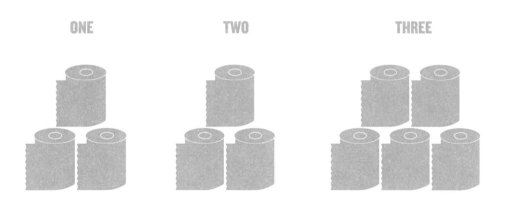

FOUR   **FIVE**   **SIX**

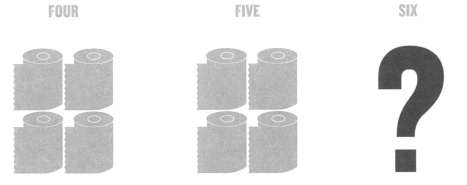

**THIS PAIR ONLY APPEARS ONCE
ON THE NEXT PAGE.**

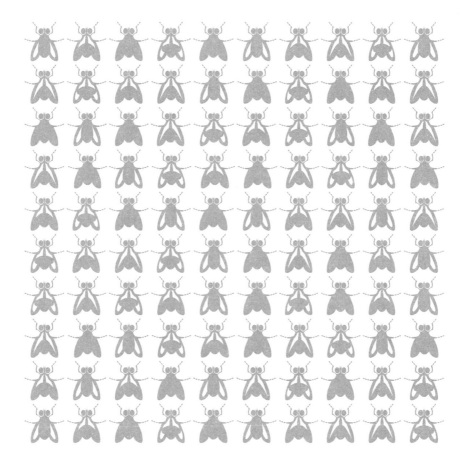

THE ROMANS USED
WATER-SOAKED SPONGES ON
THE ENDS OF STICKS INSTEAD
OF TOILET PAPER.

ON OCTOBER 25, 1760,
KING GEORGE II DIED
FALLING OFF A TOILET.

1880

1890

MR. FLY IS ON HIS LAST
LEGS. HE ONLY HAS **SIX**
FLIGHTS LEFT IN HIM.
CAN YOU HELP HIM TAKE
A NIBBLE FROM ALL
15 TURDS IN ONLY **SIX**
STRAIGHT FLIGHTS BEFORE
HE DIES?

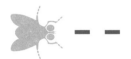

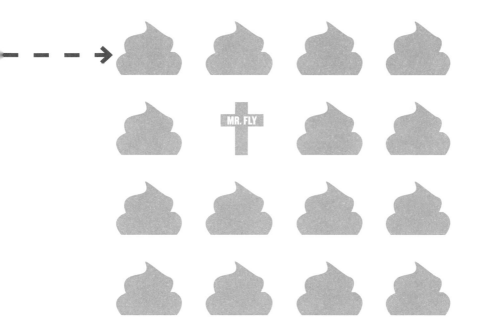

MR. FLY

SPOT THE DIFFERENCE—THERE'S ONLY ONE!

**THIS PAIR ONLY APPEARS ONCE
ON THE NEXT PAGE.**

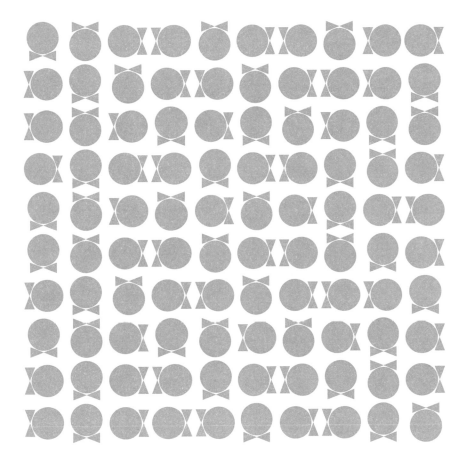

POO
FACT

3 lb/DAY

300 lb/DAY

THESE SHELVES OF
TOILET PAPER ARE
STRAIGHT. HONEST.

33% FLUSH THE TOILET WHILE SITTING ON IT.

BUM
BUTT
ARSE
BOOTY
REAR
BACKSIDE
BEHIND
BOTTOM
TUSH
RUMP

D	A	I	E	B	O	O	T	Y	U
B	R	A	B	U	M	T	F	I	B
I	S	I	A	T	I	T	B	G	E
C	E	G	C	T	S	T	O	W	H
H	I	M	K	I	R	I	T	I	I
I	T	U	S	H	T	G	T	O	N
J	A	O	I	I	L	R	O	N	D
E	I	U	D	K	V	K	M	P	M
I	P	R	E	A	R	I	W	T	S
Q	E	O	R	R	U	M	P	X	L

FARTS CONTAIN THE
FLAMMABLE GASES METHANE,
HYDROGEN SULPHIDE,
AND HYDROGEN.

THE SHAPE OF YOUR POO
DEPENDS ON THE TIME IT
HAS SPENT IN YOUR COLON.

TYPES 1 & 2 – CONSTIPATION
TYPES 3 & 4 – NORMAL
TYPE 5 – HEADING TOWARD DIARRHEA
TYPES 6 & 7 – DIARRHEA

TYPE 1
LIKE BALLS OF OVERCOOKED SAUSAGE
PASS DIFFICULTY 3
(1 EASY, 3 DIFFICULT)

TYPE 2
LIKE A LUMPY SAUSAGE
PASS DIFFICULTY 2.5

TYPE 3
LIKE A CRACKED SAUSAGE
PASS DIFFICULTY 2

TYPE 4
LIKE A SMOOTH SAUSAGE
PASS DIFFICULTY 1.5

TYPE 5

LIKE A SOFT CUT-UP SAUSAGE
PASS DIFFICULTY 1

TYPE 6

LIKE A MASHED-UP SAUSAGE
PASS DIFFICULTY 1

TYPE 7

LIKE A LIQUIDIZED SAUSAGE
PASS DIFFICULTY -4

THIS PAIR ONLY APPEARS **ONCE** ON THE NEXT PAGE.

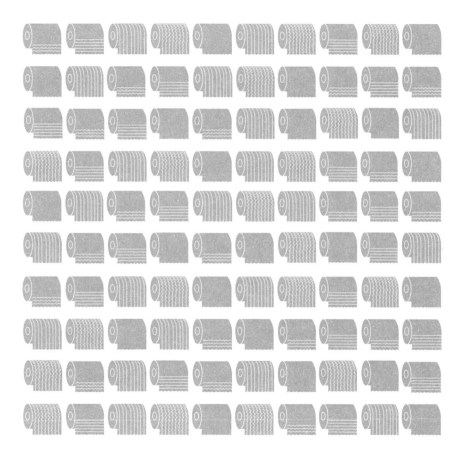

THE AVERAGE PERSON SPENDS THREE YEARS OF THEIR LIFE ON THE TOILET.

PEE

WEE

WAZ

TINKLE

URINATE

PISS

TAKE A LEAK

NUMBER ONE

A W T Z E F A P Q G
J N U M B E R O N E
I O U R I N A T E T
Y T B H P W W E E I
C U J W E Z O R A N
Y T A K E A L E A K
M P W D W S U M K L
R I E P I S S P W E
U W O V S E W A Z L
A M B Y T H W Z S M

FIND THE BABY
WITH THE DIRTY
DIAPER!

THIS PAIR ONLY APPEARS **ONCE**
ON THE NEXT PAGE.

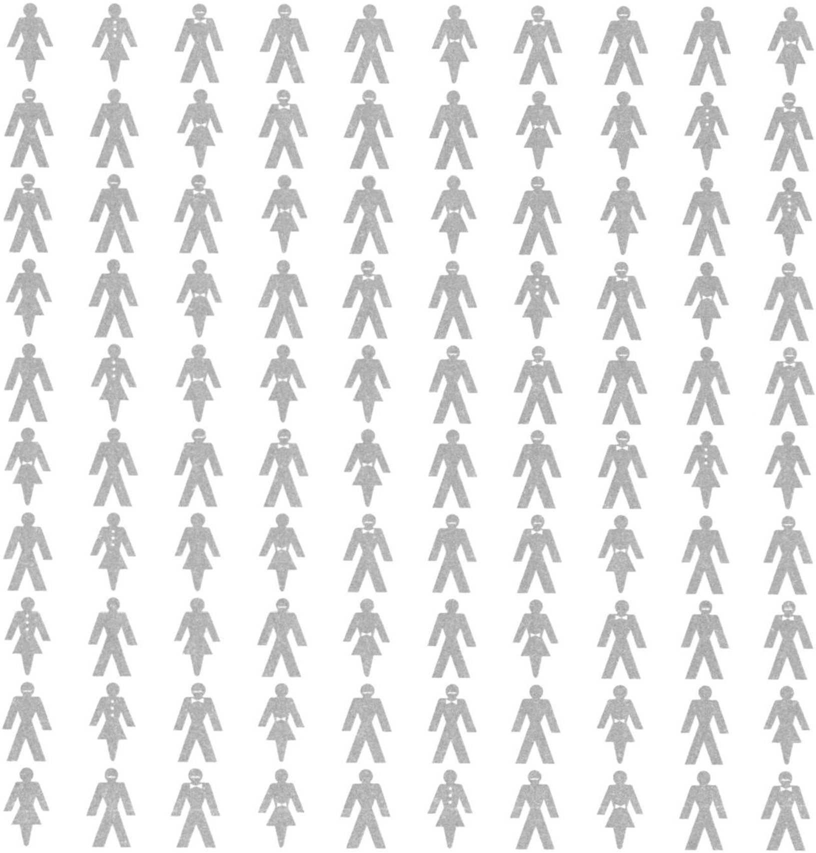

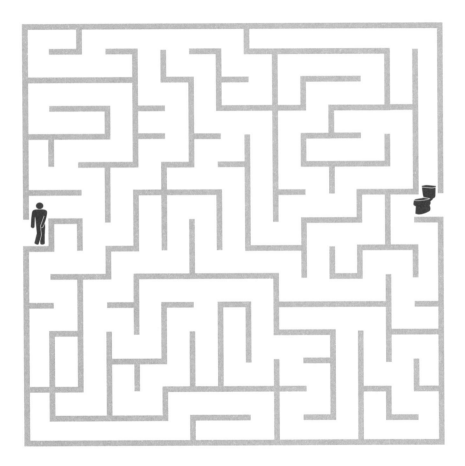

THERE CAN BE AS MANY AS
100 PARASITE EGGS,
1,000 PARASITE CYSTS,
1,000,000 BACTERIA, AND
10,000,000 VIRUSES
IN 1 GRAM OF HUMAN POO.

THE AVERAGE LENGTH OF A TWO-PLY ROLL OF TOILET PAPER IS 187 FEET.

THE AVERAGE PERSON VISITS
THE BATHROOM 2,500 TIMES
A YEAR—ABOUT SIX TO EIGHT
TIMES A DAY.

THIS PAIR ONLY APPEARS **ONCE**
ON THE NEXT PAGE.

ON AVERAGE WE EACH
USE 57 SHEETS OF TOILET
PAPER PER DAY.

ENTER
UNZIP
SIT
POO
WIPE
FLUSH
WASH
DRY
SPRAY
LEAVE

Q	V	E	N	T	E	R	E	W	V
A	W	R	I	D	L	E	A	V	E
F	A	G	P	O	O	T	S	E	O
I	S	Y	H	W	F	W	I	P	E
M	H	A	N	C	I	G	T	B	M
S	I	N	E	F	L	U	S	H	O
D	R	Y	B	I	C	N	A	H	P
E	N	I	A	P	D	Z	T	X	I
K	S	P	R	A	Y	I	O	L	U
P	S	I	U	R	T	P	U	X	L

ANSWERS

P2-3

P5

P6-7

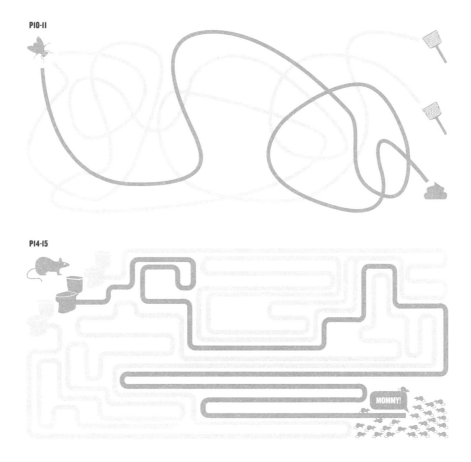

P10-11

P14-15

P20-21

F	A	E	C	E	S	D	U	M	P
H	N	L	B	E	S	R	O	U	A
S	U	C	U	X	Q	O	O	C	J
S	M	A	Q	C	R	P	T	K	B
T	B	C	C	R	A	P	Y	O	S
O	E	A	N	E	Z	I	N	P	H
O	R	R	E	M	A	N	O	O	I
L	T	G	I	E	P	G	V	O	T
E	W	H	I	N	M	A	L	I	P
F	O	T	K	T	U	R	D	M	V

P22 RAT. DROPPINGS ARE ABOUT 10MM LONG WITH BLUNT ENDS.

P23

P24-25

P30 MOUSE. SAME SIZE AS GRAINS OF RICE WITH POINTED ENDS.

P31

P36-37

```
      R   J O H N
    E               L
B   S   T D   C A N
O U T H O U S E V T
G   R   I N     A H
    O   L N     T R
    O   E Y     O O
    M   T       R N
        P R I V Y E
        K H A Z I
```

P40-41

P38-39

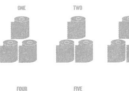

THE AMOUNT OF TOILET ROLLS IS THE NUMBER OF LETTERS IN THE WORD.

P48-49

P50-51

P54-55

P52-53

P62-63

P70-71

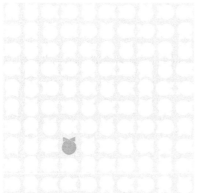

P72-73

P76-77

A W T Z E F A P Q G
J **N U M B E R O N E**
I **U R I N A T E** T
Y T B H **P** W **W E E** I
C U J **W E** Z O R A **N**
Y **T A K E A L E A K**
M P W D W S U M X **L**
R I E **P I S S** P W **E**
U W D V S E **W A Z** L
A M D Y T H W Z S M

P78-79

P80-81

P82-83

P84

P85